# HIGH PRAISE

## A BOOK OF ANTHEMS FOR UPPER-VOICE CHOIRS

*Selected & edited by Barry Rose.*

T0088305

ISBN 978-0-8536-0848-6

# NOVELLO

*part of* **WiseMusic**Group

EXCLUSIVELY DISTRIBUTED BY

Visit Hal Leonard Online at
**www.halleonard.com**

World headquarters, contact:
**Hal Leonard**
7777 West Bluemound Road
Milwaukee, WI 53213
Email: info@halleonard.com

In Europe, contact:
**Hal Leonard Europe Ltd.**
1 Red Place
London W1K 6PL
Email: info@halleonardeurope.com

In Australia, contact:
**Hal Leonard Australia Pty. Ltd.**
4 Lentara Court
Cheltenham, Victoria, 3192 Australia
Email: info@halleonard.com.au

*Cover: "The Virgin and Child with Musical Angels" (detail)*
*by Master of the Saint Bartholomew Altarpiece, active c. 1470 to 1510.*
*Reproduced by permission of The National Gallery, London.*

*Cover design: Michael Bell Design.*

*Music setting by Stave Origination.*

# PREFACE

Across the centuries composers have written music in praise of the Almighty - sometimes from moments of divine inspiration, and sometimes to order. From the huge range of church music now available for upper voices, both in and out of print, we have consciously searched for archival material, whilst also being aware of the newer musical approaches to texts we had previously associated with more traditional styles of composition.

Most choral music is about words - the music being their handmaid, so to speak, bringing them to life; and in making the choices for *High Praise* we have been aware of the educational desirability of introducing our choirs to some older texts which they may now no longer meet in modern forms of worship, as well as some newer poems and translations.

In my experience, when teaching any new piece to the choir, it is essential to begin with the text and its meaning, coupled with your own view as to the musical visions and moods the composer is seeking to create - quite a responsibility for those who run choirs. I believe that *High Praise* will present some challenges to all ranges and abilities of choirs and their directors, and, I hope, a sense of achievement and real involvement in the finished result.

So enjoy this mix of periods and styles, and happy singing!

Barry Rose
*St Albans, December 1997*

# COMPOSER INDEX

# NOTES ON THE ANTHEMS
## Barry Rose

**1. A Cradle Song - Ronald Corp** (b. 1951): well known for his work with children's choirs (The Finchley Music Group and The New London Children's Choir). This thoughtful and delicate setting is a happy marriage of words from the 18th century and music from two hundred years later. Don't take fright at what may be an unfamiliar time signature! The 7 quavers in each bar are grouped 2 + 2 + 3 and, once you and your singers are familiar with that, the cradle song will flow beautifully, creating an impression of continuous movement (as in the rocking of a cradle) through the accompaniment which, although originally conceived for piano, can be successfully played on the organ. One choral tip - you will need to work on the word 'sleep', since the letter 'P' tends not to be heard by the listeners without it being what we call 'plosive' - i.e. a *slight* explosion at the front of the lips. (Christmas; Baptism; General)

**2. Adam Lay Ybounden - Boris Ord** (1897-1961) arr. Barry Rose (b. 1934): Boris Ord's original 4-part unaccompanied setting has been a firm favourite since it was first broadcast in the 1950s in the annual Festival of Nine Lessons and Carols from the Chapel of King's College, Cambridge. This new arrangement now makes it available to upper voice choirs, whilst remaining faithful to the composer's harmony - though with a 'running' accompaniment it might be wise to sing it at a slightly steadier tempo than we usually hear in the full choir version. At bars 13-20 I suggest that there are fewer singers on the humming than on the melody. The accompaniment is suitable for either piano or organ. (Advent; Christmas)

**3. As I Outrode This Enderes Night - Gerald Hendrie** (b. 1935): written for the Choristers of Norwich Cathedral at Christmastide 1962 when Gerald Hendrie was acting-organist of the Cathedral - he accompanied the first performance with the Choristers ranged along the front of the organ loft, facing westwards toward the Nave. Rhythmic vitality and impeccable diction are essential in this carol and both conductor and choir should take great care to observe the printed dynamic markings to achieve the effect the composer intends. Good diction is a pre-requisite for any singer and it would be a wonderful practice tool to get your choir to *say* these words in the rhythm of their musical setting and see just how many *you* can hear from the back of the room/hall/church - a salutary lesson for most choirtrainers! 'Terliterlow' is a way of describing the sound made by shepherds' pipes and 'Enderes' means 'endless' (long). There is an orchestral accompaniment available, on hire from Novello, and the composer has also arranged it for four-part choir and organ (Novello), for the choir of King's College Cambridge. (Christmas)

**4. Ave, Verum Corpus (Jesu, Word Of God Incarnate) - Edward Elgar** (1857-1934): it is sometimes hard to realise that often our great composers began their careers in the most humble surroundings and Sir Edward Elgar was no exception! Born at Broadheath, Edward's father was organist of St. George's Roman Catholic Church in the nearby city of Worcester and it was for the services there that the young Elgar wrote his early compositions. *Ave Verum* (originally for 4-part choir, in the the key of G major) is one of the earliest (Opus 2) but it shows that rare melodic gift which was to imbue all of his later writing - vocal and orchestral. Throughout his life he remained a devout Catholic and would have said or sung this text in honour of the Blessed Sacrament. Although the original Latin (attributed sometimes to Pope Innocent VI) would have been sung in the Services Elgar attended, the Anglican church at that time would only allow English in its services, so an English version, to fit the music, was made. Both are included in this edition, which is an arrangement possibly by the composer himself. As in so much of Elgar's music, the phrases need to ebb and flow, perhaps with just a small hint of rubato, and great care needs to be taken over the tuning throughout and especially at bars 37, 38 and 39. The two unison sections can also sound effective when sung by a soloist or a semi-chorus.
Translation: Hail true body, born of Mary Virgin. Truly thou hast suffered, sacrificed for man on the cross. Thou, from whose pierced side flowed water and blood, be our first food in the trial of death. O merciful, O loving Jesu, son of Mary. (Communion; Maundy Thursday)

**5. And Now Another Day Is Gone - Leonard Blake** (1907-1989): Blake wrote this flowing anthem setting of Isaac Watts' poem in 1937 and a harmonised version of the melody was included in the first edition of *Hymns Ancient and Modern Revised* in 1950. As Director of Music at Malvern College and through all the work he did with the Royal School of Church Music Festivals Leonard Blake understood how to write for voices, and his music is a perfect match for the text - note the rising phrase at 'I'll sing my Maker's praise' and the descending phrase at 'I lay my body down to sleep' and the triumphant ending. A good way of achieving vocal contrast is to use a semi-chorus or an accomplished soloist in verse 2. Although marked 'Broadly' the tempo should not be too slow and it helps the word-flow if singers, director and accompanist all think 2 in a bar, rather than 4. (Evening; possible use for Memorial Services with a theme of Thanksgiving)

**6. Behold Now, Praise The Lord - William H. Harris** (1883-1973): during a lifetime spent in church music, William Harris was organist at New College, Oxford, Christ Church Cathedral, Oxford, and finally at St George's Chapel, Windsor. It was whilst he was at Windsor that he wrote *Behold Now, Praise The Lord* for the Lower Chapel Choir of Eton College, just a few minutes from Windsor, the other side of the River Thames. All of Harris' music is eminently singable and shows a real insight into superb text-setting, and especially in his anthems with words from the hymns and psalms, most of which he must have known off by heart. This is the best of Sir William - instantly memorable, strong in melodic content and with an innate understanding of what makes singers *want* to sing. The piece confounds those who hold the theory that a text which is oft repeated loses its effect - notice the number of times he sets the phrase 'give thee blessing' and how it becomes more and more effective until the final climax! Note also the time-signature - two minims in a bar - so resist the temptation to think and conduct in crotchets throughout. Although marked Voice 1 and Voice 2, it should be sung by sopranos/trebles only and definitely NOT altos. Sometimes it is performed in the key of A flat (the key in which the ATB arrangement is set - published by Novello). With some careful use of the sustaining pedal the accompaniment can be played on the piano. (General; Thanksgiving; Dedication/Patronal Feast)

**7. Christ, Whose Glory Fills The Skies - Richard Shephard** (b.1949): although the music was originally written for a soloist, Richard Shephard's setting of Charles Wesley's 'Morning Hymn' will sound well with a full unison choir, and perhaps your lower voices might like to have a 'solo' section from bars 27 to 38, with the higher voices joining in again at bar 39. When learning this piece you will find it necessary to work harder at one or two awkward corners - e.g. bars 37/8 and bars 71/2 - and then enjoy the broad and positive phrases which make up the outer verses, whilst suitably painting the words at that low lead on 'Dark and cheerless is the morn'. The accompaniment may also be played on the piano, with some possible slight realigning of parts in bars 47/8. Richard Shephard spent several years as a Lay-Vicar at Salisbury Cathedral and is now Headmaster of the Minster School at York. A prolific composer, he was also a member of the Archbishops' Commission on church music which produced the report 'In tune with Heaven'. (Morning; General; Thanksgiving)

**8. Examine Me, O Lord, And Prove Me - William Boyce** (1710-1779) arr. Watkins Shaw (1911-1996): a Chorister of St. Paul's Cathedral, Organist of St. Michael's Church, Cornhill (1736-1758) and later organist at the Chapel Royal, Boyce's works include settings of the Canticles and anthems, many of which are still sung in our cathedrals and churches. He is also remembered for editing and preparing the three volumes of *Cathedral Music* - a collection of music from various composers, published between 1760 and 1778. Boyce's music has an elegance and affecting simplicity which gives the text the prominence it should always have. In the anthem *Be thou my judge, O Lord*, it is an alto and a bass who sing 'Examine Me, O Lord, And Prove Me' but Shaw's version, which has been available since 1957, can successfully be sung by either two soprano/treble parts or soprano (treble) and alto. Be careful not to find more than one strong syllable in each bar - it's almost a case of 'thinking' one beat in a bar and taking care with such words as ex-*am*-ine, *lov*-ing and *kind*-ness. In bars 17 and 26 the vocalists should sing the same rhythm as played in the accompaniment - i.e. three equal crotchets. The tessitura of this piece is quite high for the first sopranos and needs a relaxed sound and great care over the vowel sounds at the high moments. (Lent; General)

**9. Exult** (Lord, How Great Are Thy Deeds) - **Alison Bauld** (b. 1944): Alison Bauld has chosen words which tell of the psalmist's delight in singing Jehovah's praises, and the music needs to be sung with great conviction and exultation - in what I would call a quasi-fanfare style. The flow of the text will be best communicated by using some of the tied and longer dotted notes as points for breathing or phrase breaks. Two points about diction: firstly, use the aspirate for the 'H' of 'high' (otherwise the listener may well end up hearing 'igh'); secondly, the word 'acts' is very difficult to sing well - especially when followed by a vowel - take care over this and you may end up making the smallest of breaks between 'acts' and 'O' for the sake of clarity. The small notes of the opening vocal leads (on 'Lord') should be sung on the beat and not before it. At the ends of phrases the last note often has to be shortened to accomodate the final consonant and to allow time for breathing. Four-part brass was the original choice for accompaniment (2 trumpets and 2 tenor trombones - parts available on hire), but the trumpet stops on the organ will also work well at the fanfare sections, and it is also possible to use piano throughout, or a combination of organ and piano. (General; Services of thanksgiving and celebration)

**10. Give Us The Wings Of Faith - Mark Blatchly** (b. 1960): the original text by Isaac Watts was a hymn of personal devotion - using the words 'me' and 'I', though several hymn books now use 'us' and 'we' as set here by Mark Blatchly. The music was written at my request to fill what seemed to me to be a gap in the repertoire of Saints' days anthems for high voices - its first performance was in St Albans Abbey in February 1989. You will see that there is quite a wide vocal range - nearly two octaves - but the word-setting is such that this does not present too much technical difficulty to the well-trained choir and indeed, it is possible to exploit the best qualities of your first and second sopranos/trebles at those moments of high and low writing between bars 32 and 48. This is memorable writing which expertly paints the meaning of the text, both through the vocal lines and the organ accompaniment. It needs considerable confidence from your singers and also an explanation to them that the short quaver rests are merely breathing points and not the end of the musical construction of that verse - especially in verse 1. As usual, diction is of the foremost importance, whilst keeping the smooth legato line flowing; see if you experience difficulty in hearing the words at 'and see' (bar 6), 'marked the' (bar 33), 'His zeal' (bars 36/7) - there are other similar places which will need to be worked at. When the first musical theme returns at bar 49, give it some real vocal warmth and commitment, with a gradual crescendo through the page until you reach the four-part ending. Piano accompaniment is possible, but the effect is much better on the organ. (Any Saint's Day)

**11. How Blest Are They That Fear The Lord - Stephen Oliver** (1950-1992): when asked to write an anthem for the wedding scene in the Royal Shakespeare Company's production of Nicholas Nickleby, Stephen Oliver went back to his musical roots as a chorister at St Paul's Cathedral and chose a text from one of the Psalms (128) associated with the Marriage Service and which the composer had sung many times as a treble. Eschewing his own naturally inventive and original style, he consciously wrote in a style to suit the period in which the play is set and in the original production a recording of the anthem by the boys of St Paul's Cathedral was played each night in the show. The composer later added a second verse so that we might use it as a more extended anthem at the boys-only Evensong in St Paul's each Monday. The singing requires a good sense of a sustained line and pitch - it is easy in a piece such as this for the ends of phrase to 'sag' and cause the odd pitch problem. Deep breathing is a pre-requisite and diction needs to be worked at - it is not easy to sing successfully 'feareth the' (bars 35 and 39) and the whole point of having this text is lost if great care is not taken over finishing the word 'wife' (bar 19) correctly. I have heard performances where all we have heard is 'wi...'! Originally scored for organ, this may also be played on the piano with extra care at bars 32/33. (Weddings; General)

**12. I Will Sing Of Thy Great Mercies - Felix Mendelssohn-Bartholdy** (1809-1847): here is an aria from the oratorio, *St Paul* which Mendelssohn wrote when he was in his early twenties. It was first performed, in its original German text, on 22 May 1836 in Dusseldorf. The oratorio tells of the martyrdom of Stephen, Saul's persecution of the church, his conversion on the road to Damascus and, as Paul, his preaching of God's word with Barnabas. *I Will Sing Of Thy Great Mercies* is preceded by a recitative, but since that is part of the on-going story we have omitted it here and added a four bar introduction which now makes this useful as a choir anthem or solo aria. Mendelssohn had the gift of writing beautiful tunes and this is one of them - so enjoy singing it and look as though you are enjoying it. Choir directors should take care NOT to conduct all three quavers in the bar - it is better to imagine the musical construction as 2 + 1 and try to convey that to your singers. The accompaniment is equally suited to piano or organ. (General; Feasts of St Barnabas and/or St Paul)

**13. I Will Worship Toward Thy Holy Temple - George Dyson** (1883-1964): a native of Halifax, West Yorkshire, George Dyson (later to become Sir George) went on to become a student at the Royal College of Music, returning there as its Director from 1937-1952. Like so many of his contemporaries, he grew up under the influence of music in church and for a time was an organist in Greenwich. Although considered as one of the more 'conservative in style' composers, his music has a natural melodic flow and an obvious affinity with the texts he set. Dyson loved the language of the liturgy, and especially the psalms, though there are some disagreements between the text he set and the text he would have found in his prayer book, possibly because he was setting it from memory. From the performer's angle it is often useful to remind ourselves and our singers that a 6/8 time signature implies just the two (dotted crotchet) beats in each bar and that helps the music to flow with a lilt. The singers will find that the word 'toward' will need to become just the one syllable - 'tward'. Note that we have taken the editorial liberty of adding the word 'and' at the beginning of bar 48 and repeating the word 'yet' at the beginning of bar 54. (General)

**14. Light Of The World - John Dankworth** (b. 1927): both the text and the music were specially written for inclusion in *Worship Songs Ancient and Modern*. Paul Wigmore is one of the most highly regarded modern hymn writers whilst John Dankworth is internationally known as a jazz musician though he had previously written music for the church, including a setting of the Mass. Here the text is beautifully matched by a flowing melody, with its effective change of key at 'Light of the world', and is suitable as a solo, choir anthem, or for use as a hymn. Some of the phrases might seem to be rather long for younger voices and it is possible to help the sense of the text by taking a small break (breath) after 'life' in bar 41 and also after 'lost' (but only on the second time round) in bar 19. Although originally conceived for piano, the accompaniment is also well suited to the organ or guitar. (General)

**15. Magnificat and Nunc Dimittis in G - John Wood** (d. ca. 1989): there are several occasions throughout the year when Evensong at our cathedrals and greater churches is sung by visiting school choirs, and we hope that you will find the inclusion of a setting of the Canticles and a set of treble voice Responses to be useful. This setting of the *Evensong Canticles* was written in 1956 and contrasts a spirited and tuneful Magnificat against a thoughtful and flowing Nunc Dimittis - both using the same music to the Gloria. Note the time signature of two minims in the Magnificat and the Gloria and avoid any tendency to sing (or conduct) in crotchet beats since this will give you the wrong word stresses. It is also important for the accompanist to observe the composer's phrase marks since there may be a tendency to play too staccato or pointed a rhythm in the Magnificat. In the Nunc Dimittis remember that a 9/8 time signature indicates just the three beats in a bar and that is the way it should always be conducted. The duplets (bars 7, 9 and 10) are easy to manage and make an effective contrast to the flowing phrases elsewhere, though you may have to do some careful rehearsing over the length of the last note of bar 7 ('pre...'). The second vocal part is in a comfortable range for those who usually sing alto and the accompaniment works with either piano or organ. John Wood was a pupil of the late Herbert Sumsion at Gloucester Cathedral and spent his musical life in Devon as organist and choirmaster at Broadclyst, Crediton and Woodbury Parish churches. [Unfortunately, we have been unable to trace his dates and would welcome this information.]

**16. Make Me A Light - Philip Wilby** (b. 1949): written for a junior choir, here is a worship-song which will immediately appeal to your younger singers - or it could be used with equal effectiveness as an anthem with a full refrain and with verses sung by soloists. With its recurring theme of bringing light it needs to be sung with a radiant smile, something which young children often seem to do much better than adults! The tune is memorable and perfectly matched to the words and your more experienced junior or adult singers will enjoy putting in the 'ad lib extra voices', perhaps in the refrain after the third verse. The accompaniment is equally suited to piano, organ or guitar. (General; Advent; Christingle Services; Candelmas)

**17. Mater Ora Filium - Charles Wood** (1866-1926) arr. Harrison Oxley (b. 1933): when Charles Wood completed his version of *Mater Ora Filium* in 1917 he acknowledged that the attractive melody was 'based on an Irish folk-song'. Like me, I suspect that Harrison Oxley knew this version from singing classes at school, and he has since arranged it most beautifully for soloists, accompanying two-part choir and organ, though you will see that he has also given other options as to how the voices may be distributed. With the use of two different languages (and it might inform, or amuse your choir to know that the term is 'macaronic') it is important that a lot of care is paid to diction and the meaning of the words. As with all Latin texts, the length of the vowels is important and Mr. Oxley has given you a guide to some of these. Be careful to voice the 'N' of the end of the word 'Bairn', (otherwise the listener hears 'bear'!) and get your choir to read the text out before they sing in order to get used to the unusual style of the words. The instruction of 'Two or Three Voices' at bar 53 is very important, since descants often have a habit of drowning the melody - rather than decorating it. The 'open hum' at bars 69-72 will need some practice - a good way to do it is to start rehearsing with lips together (as in 'm') and continue singing whilst pulling the lips apart - that will give the singers a guide to the sensation and sound they need to aim for at this point.
Translation: Mother, pray to your son that, after this exile, he will give us the joy of all the blessèd. (Christmas; Epiphany)

**18. My Song Is In Sighing - Martin Dalby** (b. 1942): written on 2 October 1964, just after the composer had finished his studies with Herbert Howells at the Royal College of Music. This anthem not only shows the fruits of that study but also reflects the earlier musical influences on Martin Dalby - his father, who was organist of St. Machar's Cathedral, Aberdeen, and his singing as a boy chorister at St. Mary's Episcopal Church, Aberdeen. He was later to become Head of Music for BBC Scotland - a post he held from 1972-1991. The text is part of a longer poem by Richard Rolle and is the yearning of someone who seeks and longs for Christ to come into their life. It needs to be sung with great affection for the words and if sung by a group (it is also suitable as a solo) it would be a good idea to have the words read aloud before doing any singing. Keep a beautiful legato line and be careful not to sing the weaker syllables too strongly in words such as *sigh*-ing, *lang*-ing, *shin*-ing etc. The accompaniment is also suitable for piano but you will need to take care with the widely-spread chords in bars 36, 37 and 38. (General; also suitable as a Communion motet during Lent and times of supplication)

**19. O Bone Jesu - Richard Dering** (or Deering) (c.1580-1630): although he was born and died in England, Dering spent much of his time studying and working abroad, in Italy and in Belgium, where he was an organist at the convent of English nuns in Brussels. His music is clearly influenced by the Italian style of the period in which solo voices often played a leading role, either singly or in duet, accompanied by either harpsichord or organ with basso continuo. *O Bone Jesu* is a personal prayer of supplication and the musical keywords must be 'sustained tone' and 'deep breathing'. The phrases are often quite long so it is important that, though the tempo is solemn, it should never be allowed to sag - perhaps a useful metronome guide would be minim = 60. Although usually sung by two tenors, it is also well suited to the sound of two soprano/treble parts (NOT soprano/ treble and alto) and it is important that your singers familiarise themselves with the sound of the Latin vowels, and especially the opening phrase, which can sound very 'Anglican' with the incorrect pronounciation of 'O' of 'bone' - make sure this vowel is not too open. This fine modern edition is by Richard Charteris of the University of Sydney in Australia.

Translation: O good Jesu, O sweet Jesu, O Jesu, son of Mary Virgin, full of mercy and love, according to thy great mercy have mercy on me. (Ash Wednesday; Lent; Passiontide)

**20. O Magnum Mysterium - Giles Swayne** (b. 1946): the text is the first phrase of a Responsory set for the Office of Matins on Christmas Day and it tells of the great mystery of seeing our Lord laid in a cradle amongst the oxen. The music, written specifically for Gordon Roland-Adams and the boys at Westminster Under School (where the composer's son was a pupil), brings to life that mystery in Giles Swayne's individual, inventive and challenging style. Like all successful choir directors, you will need to acquaint yourself thoroughly with the note values, rhythms and musical construction before you present it to your singers - note that the one-bar instrumental interjection at bar 22 uses the notes of the first vocal section in the order in which they have been sung and also the reverse order in which they are sung between bars 23 and 32. There are places where the harmony seems to be in four parts, but a closer examination will reveal that very rarely is that fourth part not being doubled by one of the other parts. The composer is specific about the basic beat being a quaver and for learning purposes it might be a useful time-saver and confidence builder to learn the parts at separate rehearsals until they are reasonably fluent and then put them together - you, and the singers, should be delighted at the effect. Be careful not to hurry in bars 27/28/29, the notes are short and the singers often tend to rush in after silences. Also take care to observe the composer's stress marks, so that the correct syllable of the word is emphasised - as in mys-TE-ri (see bar 2 etc.). The last consonant of that word needs to be sung where the letter 'M' is printed. This is a piece which will repay all the work you will need to do on it and bring this quite well-known text to life in a new and innovative way. (Christmas)

Translation: O great mystery and wonderful sacrament, that the animals were able to see the new-born Lord... Alleluia!

**21. The Cradle In Bethlehem - Roger Quilter** (1877-1953): born in Brighton and educated at Eton College, Roger Quilter studied composition in Germany and is now best remembered as the composer of *The Children's Overture* and some melodious and well-crafted songs. *The Cradle In Bethlehem* began life as a solo song and, although we are including the two-part arrangement, it might be a good idea to have the first verse sung as it was originally written - with a soloist or semi-chorus singing just the melody. Just as effective would be to have that same solo or semi-chorus effect in verse 2, but now using both parts of the harmony. From then on the full choir could sing (from bar 23) thus creating a different vocal texture. The juxtaposition of the duplets against the rest of the bar (i.e. bars 5, 15, 18 etc.) may need some careful work - and it might help the singers if it is explained to them that the composer was merely trying to give the words at this point their proper prominence and inflection, and the singers a chance to pronounce them properly. As the metronome mark indicates, always think of 6/8 music as two beats in the bar - like the gentle rocking of a cradle the composer is trying to recreate. The accompaniment may also be played successfully on the organ. (Christmas)

**22. The Lamb - Henry Walford Davies** (1869-1941): *The Lamb*, with its text by William Blake, is the first of *Four Songs of Innocence*, an early work for female voices by Davies and written for the students whilst he was teaching composition at the Royal College of Music. He was later to go on to be Organist of the Temple Church (1898-1923) and become the first Religious Music Adviser to the BBC from 1927 until his death. This is one of those pieces where the phrases need to ebb and flow with much graciousness and with a hint of rubato, despite the rhythmic figurations in the original piano accompaniment from bar 7 onwards. The balance between the three parts is important, though each has its own 'solo' phrases which need a warm and characterful sound. The complete ensemble is sparingly used and thus gives an extra warmth and effect at those moments. One practical point: 1st sopranos/trebles should get a good breath after 'life' (bar 7) since the rest of the phrase is quite long - we have marked in an editorial breathing 'carry-over' at bar 8. (Baptism; Children's Services; now associated with Christmas)

**23. Praise The Lord - Carol Barratt** (b. 1945): the festive text of Psalm 150 has been set in many styles over the centuries, and here is a new setting of the translation from the Alternative Service Book. Some choir directors may be deterred by a 5/4 time signature, but some careful study of the musical construction of this piece will show the grouping of the crotchets, i.e. 2 + 3 (as in the opening refrain) or 3 + 2 (as in 'Praise his strength in heaven') and this indicates the way you should conduct it. It would be wise for choir directors/conductors to work all this out before the first rehearsal with their choir. In my experience, children are far quicker to master these rhythms than some of us oldies! Be careful not to set too fast a speed (the composer indicates 'moderato') but do get your choir to sing decisively and with a facial expression that also shows that here is an anthem of real praise! Experienced choir directors will know that not all note values are sung as printed - i.e. the first 'praise' must be shortened to make the point of the repeated 'praise', and so on, throughout the piece. [This may be the opportunity for me to remind us all that the letter 'D' (as at the end of 'Lord') is one of those letters which can sound like a 'T' to the listeners. A quick rule-of-thumb which is understood by singers of *all* ages is that you *sing* a 'D' and *say* a 'T' - try a descending scale alternating 'God' and 'Gott' and see what I mean.] Originally written for piano accompaniment, this setting is also suited to the organ, though the repeated chords will need to be very clearly articulated. There is also a brass quintet arrangement (by Tony Small) available (on hire from Novello) for orchestral instruments (2 trumpets, horn in F or trumpet 3, trombone and tuba or bass trombone) or brass band instruments (2 cornets, E flat horn, euphonium and E flat bass). (General; Services of thanksgiving and celebration)

**24. Prevent Us, O Lord - Derek Holman** (b.1931): if it were not for their use in anthem settings by such composers as William Byrd and from this century, Alan Ridout and Derek Holman (both included in this book), these lovely words would probably remain unknown to many singers. They come from the Order of Ordination of Priests and Deacons in the Book of Common Prayer. In the mid 1950s Derek Holman was running the choir at St Stephen's Church, Rochester Row, Westminster, London and his vicar was the Reverend George Reindorp, later to become Bishop of Guildford and then Bishop of Salisbury. In those days several of the London churches had boys in their choir and it was for the boys at St Stephen's that this setting was written. It is a miniature of exquisite craftmanship and musical taste and perfectly catches the meaning and flow of the words. That flow is best maintained if the conductor thinks of 2 + 2 in the bar, rather than the four crotchets shown in the time signature. Note the word-painting at 'glorify' and the mysterious mood created by the organ/piano as it takes us towards the words which point us to the life beyond death 'and finally...'. Be careful at this point (bars 23 and 24) not to have too many stressed syllables and also to make sure that your choir 'voices' (i.e. sings) the letter 'B' in 'obtain'. (General: Ordination; End of Term Services)

**25. Prevent Us, O Lord** - **Alan Ridout** (1934-1996): for details of the text, please see Derek Holman's setting of the same words (no. 24). Originally written for the choir of a girls' school (SSAA), it is also possible to sing this with two soprano/treble parts, altos on the third line down, and tenors at the bottom of the four-part setting. Alan Ridout's music has a sonority and fervour which shows an innate understanding of the text for which he was writing and I often liken the first entry of all four parts (bar 12 onwards) to a gradual opening of a beautiful fan. Your singers will need a good sense of legato singing and to be able to capture the expressive moments at 'that in all our works' (begun by whoever is singing the third line down). Some careful learning and rehearsal in tuning is necessary at bars 36-45, and it might be useful for those singing the *second* part down to learn their part first of all - especially that awkward moment from bars 44/45. Take care to observe the dynamics from bar 48 onwards, so that the intensity is built up as the text repeats itself ('through Jesus Christ our Lord') and all must quieten down for the mysterious and hushed ending. In its modern everyday context 'Prevent' means to stop, but in this context it means 'go before' or 'guide' - and the first syllable is usually sung as *Pree* and not *Pri*. The accompaniment is suitable for organ or piano. (Ordination; End of Term Services; General)

**26. Risen Lord** - **Barry Rose** (b. 1934): the first time I saw these words was on a beautifully calligraphed card affixed to our Precentor's pantry door in St. Albans, and the music was specially written for a Sunday-School act of worship which took place in the Abbey Refectory on Good Friday, 1989. Just one word will describe the musical approach you should take: cheerful; and not only should that apply to the sound but also to the way the singers look! It is surprising how many choirs look miserable when singing texts of such a positive nature. The original version was just one unison verse, but I have produced this extended version for *High Praise* together with a short introduction. Keep the music moving at two beats to the bar and be especially careful over the words beginning with the letter 'L' - 'Lord', 'Love', 'laughter' since 'L' is one of those letters which tends to be under-sung - your singers need to use their tongues properly to make it sound clear to the listeners. The accompaniment was originally played on a digital piano, but it also suits the organ, with or without pedals. The Reverend John Hencher teaches at Monmouth School and lives in Herefordshire. (Easter; Communion; General)

**27. The Blessed Virgin's Cradle Song** - **Edward Bairstow** (1874-1946): I have always felt that a primary duty of the choir director is to spend time exploring the text with his/her singers, either before or just after an initial sing-through of the piece. In this carol you will find words such as 'kine' (cows) and 'pang' (pain) which are now not in common everyday use and an explanation of their meaning (and perhaps that this was the accepted liturgical language of the time) will make your singers feel more at ease with them. Edward Bairstow (later to become Sir Edward Bairstow of York Minster) wrote the music at Wigan Parish Church in 1899, the words having been written by a curate at the church, the Reverend Edgar Rogers. The flowing melodic lines lie beautifully within a comfortable vocal range - ideally soprano/treble and alto - and the accompaniment is suited to both piano and organ, though it may be necessary to spread some of the chords on the piano. It goes without saying that lullabies are gentle and perhaps it might be an idea to begin the first verse with a semi-chorus of those singers who can manage the quiet start. The rest of the choir might then come in at 'Love shall be thy cradle'. Although it is not marked, I think the choir should divide equally at 'Slumber in thy manger'. Beware in verse 1! You will need a small break at the comma after 'Lying' - otherwise the sense of the words will become totally wrong! (Christmas)

**28. Preces and Responses** - **Stephen Darlington** (b.1952): *High Praise* now offers you the one remaining musical element needed for your Service of Evensong (or Matins) - the setting of the Responses by Stephen Darlington. Currently Director of Music at Christ Church, Oxford, Stephen Darlington was Master of Music at the Cathedral and Abbey Church of St Alban from 1978 to 1985, having previously been Assistant Organist of Canterbury Cathedral. This setting of the Responses was written for the St Albans Choristers, Evensong between Monday and Friday being sung by the Choristers alone. Suitable for SSS or SSA, you may find it easier to learn these with the individual parts, rather than at a concerted rehearsal, and when that is done it is useful to get the two lower parts to rehearse together, adding the top line later. In some ways, it is the second trebles who need to be the most confident since they often complete the chords, especially at the ends of phrases. You will find that each line is quite melodic, though your singers will surely enjoy the slight dissonances produced at 'Lord/Christ have mercy upon us'. The priest's part may be sung at the printed pitch or an octave higher (by a woman priest or a member of your choir) and, if absolutely necessary, there could be a quiet accompaniment to the Responses until the choir are really sure of them.

[Note: While the ordering of the anthems in this book is basically alphabetical by title, the order has been adjusted to allow two 2-page anthems (nos. 5 and 24) to be printed as single 'spreads'.]

# 1. A CRADLE SONG

Text
William Blake

RONALD CORP
(b. 1951)

Sweet sleep, with soft down Weave thy brows an in - fant crown.

Sweet sleep,— An - gel mild, Ho - ver o'er my hap - - py

child.

div. a 3    rall.    a tempo

Sleep, sleep,— hap - py child, All cre - a - tion slept and smil'd;

e - ver \_\_ see, Heaven - ly face that smiles on thee,

Smiles on thee, on me, on all; Who be-came an in - fant small.

In - fant smiles are His own \_ smiles; Heav'n and earth to peace \_ be -

- guiles.

# 2. ADAM LAY YBOUNDEN

Text
Anon
15th Century

BORIS ORD
(freely arranged by Barry Rose*)

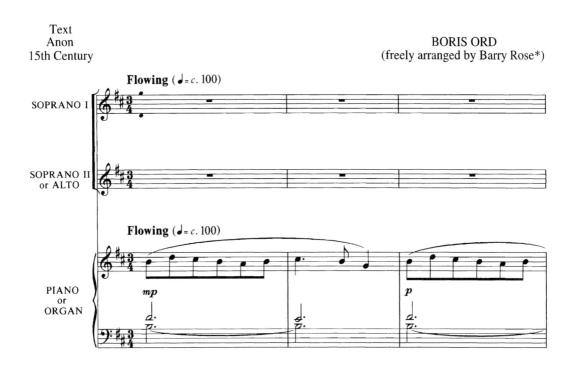

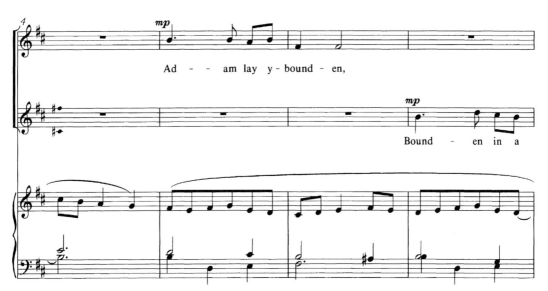

*\* For St. Albans Abbey Girls Choir*

6

Four thou - sand win - ter Thought he not too

bond: Four thou - sand win - - ter Thought he not too__

long. *(Hum)* mm _____

long. And all was for an ap - ple, an ap - - ple that he

took, As clerk - ès find - en writ-ten in their book.

mm _____

sempre **mp**

sempre **p**

sempre **f**

*For the choristers of Norwich Cathedral*

# 3. AS I OUTRODE THIS ENDERES NIGHT

Words
Traditional

GERALD HENDRIE
(b. 1935)

*In which case, omit *l.h.* chords and play small notes instead.

© Copyright 1964 Novello & Company Limited
This edition © Copyright 1997 Novello & Company Limited

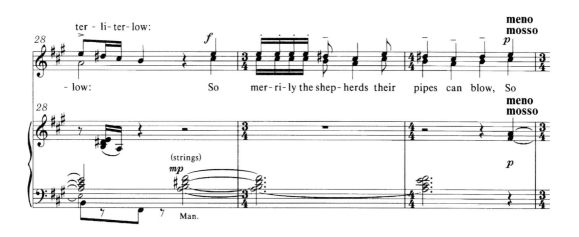

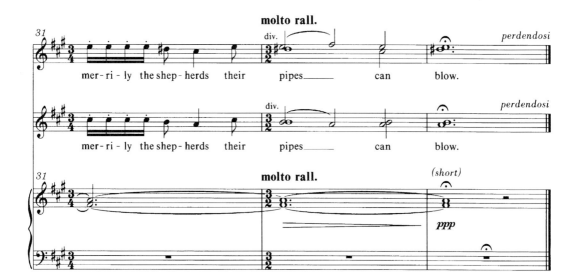

# 4. AVE VERUM CORPUS
## JESU, WORD OF GOD INCARNATE

Text
14th-century hymn

EDWARD ELGAR
(1857 - 1934)

# 5. AND NOW ANOTHER DAY IS GONE

Text
Isaac Watts

LEONARD BLAKE
(1907-1989)

head, And through the hours of dark - ness_ keep Their watch a - round my

bed. With cheer - ful heart I_

close my eyes, Since_ Thou wilt not re - move, And in the morn - ing

let me_ rise Re - joic - ing, re - joic - - ing in Thy love.

18

*For Julian Lambart and the Eton College Lower Chapel Choir*

# 6. BEHOLD, NOW, PRAISE THE LORD

Text
Psalm 134

WILLIAM H. HARRIS
(1883-1973)

22

# 7. CHRIST, WHOSE GLORY FILLS THE SKIES

Text
Charles Wesley

RICHARD SHEPHARD
(b.1949)

*Written for the Rediffusion Chorister Competition 1981.*

night; Day-spring from on high, be near; Day___ star,

In my heart___ ap - - pear.

**a little slower**

Dark and cheer-less is the morn Un - ac -

- com - pan - ied by Thee; Joy - less is the day's re-

turn till thy mer - cies beams I see Till they

in - ward light im - part, Glad my eyes, and warm my

heart. Vis - - it then this

soul of mine, Pierce the gloom of sin and grief;

Fill me Ra - dian - cy Di - vine, Scat - ter all my

un - be - lief. More and more Thy self dis -

- play, shin - - - ing shin - - -

- ing to the per - fect day.

# 8.  EXAMINE ME, O LORD

Text
Psalm xxvi, 2-3

WILLIAM BOYCE
(1710-1779)
arr. Watkins Shaw

From the Anthem *Be thou my judge*. Originally for Alto and Bass, a major seventh lower, in $\frac{3}{2}$ time.

[* *] At these points, the original bass vocal part was the same as the instrumental bass.

*for Florrie and Alex*

# 9. EXULT

Text
Psalm 92

ALISON BAULD
(b. 1944)

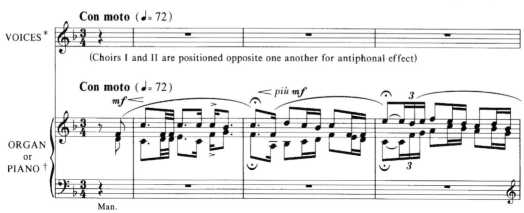

(Choirs I and II are positioned opposite one another for antiphonal effect)

*Commissioned by Pipers Corner School to celebrate its Diamond Jubilee, 1990.*

© Copyright 1997 Novello & Company Limited

\* This anthem may be sung by one choir divided into two parts and using soloists, or it may be sung by two choirs.
In some places Choir I divides into two parts, while Choir II remains unison throughout - except at bb. 45-7 where either
the top or bottom part may be sung.

† The original version for brass quartet is available on hire.

\* 8va and 8va bassa for piano performances only.

of a ten stringed lute___ to the sound-ing chor(ds)___ of a har(p)___

___ Thy Acts O Lord___ fill me with ex - ul - ta - tion___ I shout! in

tri-umph___ at thy migh-ty deeds

CHOIR II

How great are thy deeds___ O Lord___ it is

34

good to give thee thanks___ to sing psalms to thy name O most High___

CHOIR I

div.

thy migh - ty deeds___

Thy acts O Lord    fill me with ex - ul - ta - tion___

Ped.

poco rit.

fill me with ex - ul - ta - tio(n),___ Thy Acts O Lord O most High.

Thy Acts O Lord O most High.

poco rit.

* The anthem may end here.

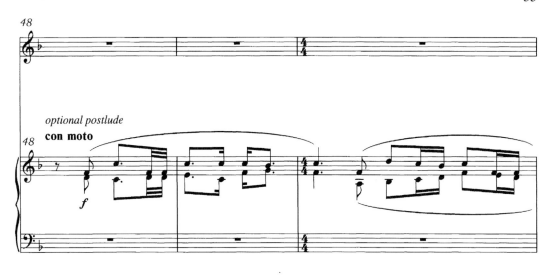

*optional postlude*
**con moto**

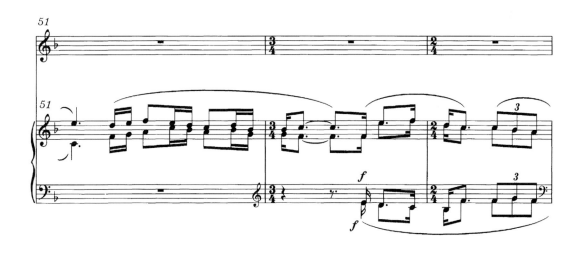

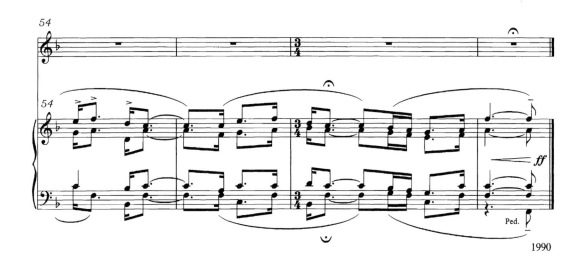

# 10. GIVE US THE WINGS OF FAITH

Text
Isaac Watts

MARK BLATCHLY
(b.1960)

Give us the wings of faith_____ to rise_____ With-in the

veil,_____ and see The saints a - bove, how great____ their

Joys,_____ how great____ their joys

how bright___ their glo - ries, their glo - ries be.___

June 1988

40

*To Trevor Nunn*

# 11. HOW BLEST ARE THEY THAT FEAR THE LORD

### Wedding Anthem

Text
Psalm 128

STEPHEN OLIVER
(1950 - 1992)

# 12. I WILL SING OF THY GREAT MERCIES

(St. Paul)

Text
Psalm lxxxix 1.

FELIX MENDELSSOHN-BARTHOLDY
(1809-1847)

Con moto (♪= 92)

VOICES

I will sing of Thy great mer - cies, O Lord, of Thy mer-cies, O Lord, my Sa - - - viour, I will sing of Thy great mer - cies, O Lord, and of Thy faith - - - ful - ness e - ver

*40*

Lord,       and of Thy faith-ful - ness   ev -  -  - er  more,

*45*

and   of  Thy   faith-ful - ness   ev -  -  er  more,

*mf*

*50*

ev -  -  -  -  -  -  er  more,       ev -  -  -

*dim.*   *p*   *mf*   *dim.*

*55*

-  -  - er  more.

*p*

# 13. I WILL WORSHIP

Text
Psalm cxxxviii,
vv. 2, 4, 5, 6, 7

GEORGE DYSON
(1883 - 1964)

kind - ness, for thy lov - - - ing - kind - ness and truth.

All the kings of the earth shall

praise thee, they shall sing in the ways of the

Lord, that great is the glo - ry, that

For though the

Lord___ is___ high,___ Yet hath he re-

-spect un-to the low - - ly;___ and though I

49

**largamente**

walk ___ in the midst ___ of trou - ble, ___ yet thou shalt re-

**calando**

- fresh me, yet thou shalt re - fresh me and thy right hand ___

___ shall hold me, shall hold me,

shall hold me. ___

# 14. LIGHT OF THE WORLD

Text
Paul Wigmore

JOHN DANKWORTH
(b. 1927)

WAVENDON

2nd time to CODA ⊕

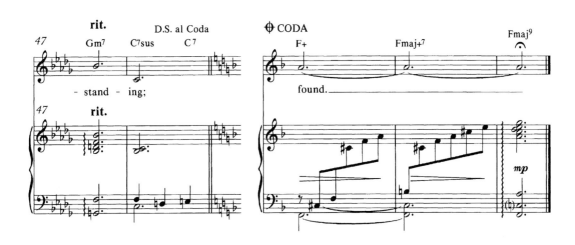

*To D.R.A.P.*

# 15. MAGNIFICAT and NUNC DIMITTIS

in G major

JOHN WOOD

Magnificat

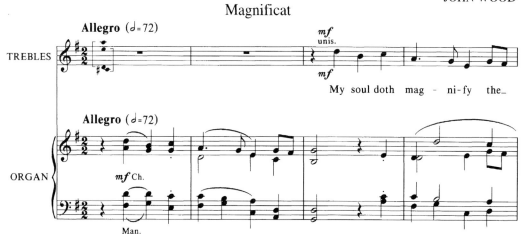

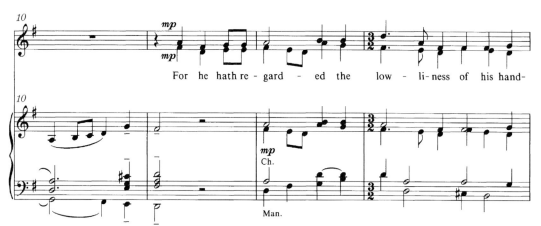

fear___ him through-out all___ ge - ne - ra - tions.

He hath shew - ed strength with his arm: he hath scat-tered the

Man.

proud in the i - ma - gi - na - tion of their hearts.

proud in the i - ma - gi - na-tion of their___ hearts. He hath

put down the migh - ty___ from their seat: and hath ex-

Man.

-al - ted the hum - ble and meek. He hath filled the hun - gry with

good things: and the rich he hath sent__ emp - ty a - way. He re -

- mem-b'ring his mer - cy hath hol-pen his ser - vant Is - ra-el: as he__

pro - mised to our fore - fa - thers, A - bra-ham and__ his seed, for__ e - ver.

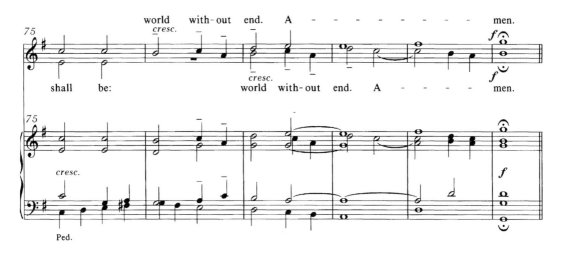

## NUNC DIMITTIS

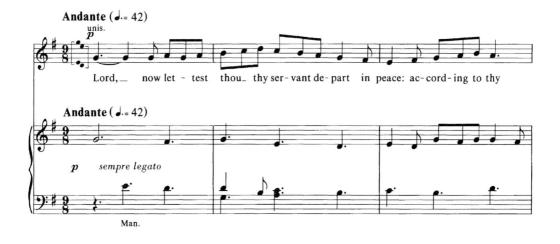

cresc. poco a poco

unis.

thou hast____ pre - pared be-fore the face of all peo - ple; To be a

light____ to ligh-ten the Gen - tiles: and to be__ the

glo - ry of thy peo - - ple Is - ra - el.

Man.

Gloria as before
(Page 58)

*For St. Peter's Junior Choir*

# 16. MAKE ME A LIGHT

Words and music by
PHILIP WILBY
(b. 1949)

† Optional countermelody last (4th) time only

* Ad lib. extra voices

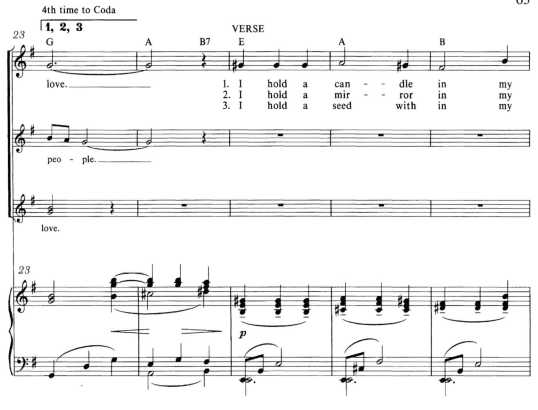

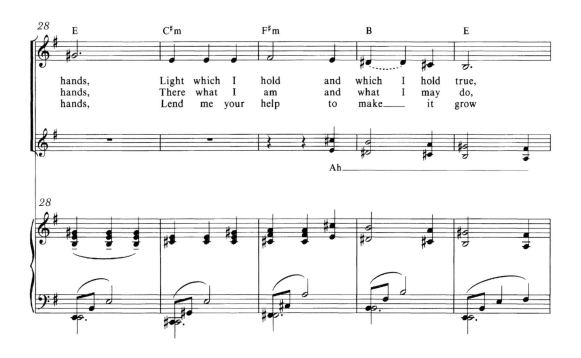

64

*For St Edmundsbury Cathedral Girls Choir in its tenth anniversary year*

# 17. MATER ORA FILIUM

Text
Anon. 15th Century

CHARLES WOOD
(1866-1926)
arr. Harrison Oxley

*Ideally, the singer of the Solo I part should be placed apart from the choir. This singer should not sing in unison with the choir except for the 8 bars marked 'All voices'. The singers of Solo II and Solo III should be drawn from among the choir. However, this arrangement of the parts is entirely at the conductor's discretion and may be modified at will. For example, any of the solo parts may be sung full or by a group of voices.

†The organ part may be performed on the piano if some tied notes are repeated and some chords spread.

SOLO III
*mf*
That thou bear - est in thine arm? Sir, it is a King - es Son

Ped.

TWO or THREE VOICES
*p hum with lips slightly apart*
er

FULL
*mf*
That in heav'n a - bove doth won. 2. Man to Fa - ther he hath none,

*(mp) legato*

er                    er

But him - self God a - lone; Of a maid he would be born, To

save man-kind that was for-lorn. **ALL VOICES** *Ma - ter o - ra fi - li - um,*

*Ut post hoc ex - il - i - um No - bis do - net gau - di - um,*

*Be - a - to - rum om - ni - um.*

Man.

SOLO I tacet

3. Three kings brought him pre - sents,— Gold,— myrrh, and frank - in - cense,

*mp legato*

41

To my Son full of might, King of kings and Lord of right.

45 SOLO I
*mf*

Ma - ter o - ra fi - li - um, Ut post hoc ex - il - i - um

*div.*

ah _____ ah _____

Ped.

49 *f* _____ *mf*

No - bis do - net gau - di - um, Be - a - to - rum om - ni - um.

ah _____

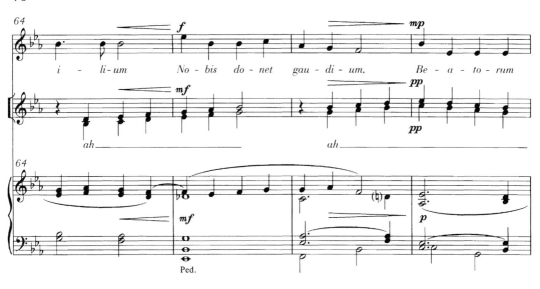

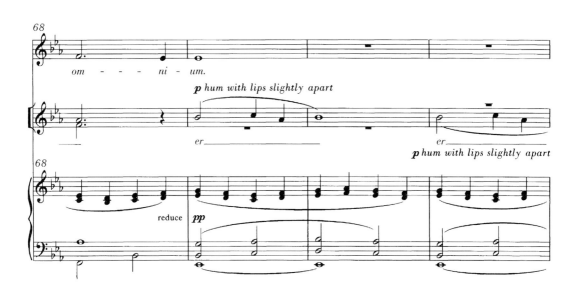

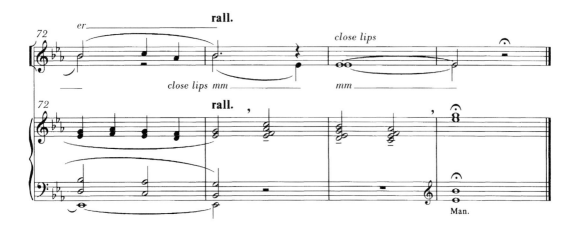

# 18. MY SONG IS IN SIGHING

Text
Richard Rolle

MARTIN DALBY
(b.1942)

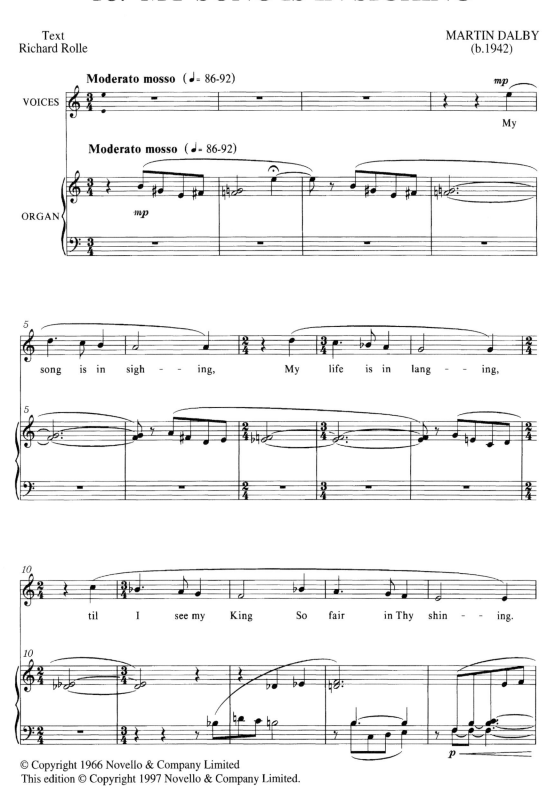

So fair in Thy fair - - head; in - til Thy light me lead, and in Thy love me feed: In love make me to speed that Thou be ev - er my meed. When

fairhead: beauty    meed: reward

*cantabile*

cover: recover

# 19. O BONE JESU

RICHARD DERING (c. 1580-1630)
Transcribed, edited and realised by
Richard Charteris

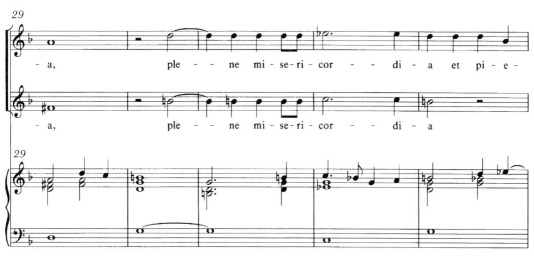

mi - se - re - re me - - - - - i,

-i, mi - se - re - re me - - - - i,

O bo - ne Je - su, O dul - cis Je - su,

O bo - ne Je - su, O dul - cis Je - su, se - cun - dum

se - cun - dum ma - gnam mi - se - ri -

ma - gnam mi - se - ri - cor - di - am tu - - am,

*to Gordon Roland*

# 20. O MAGNUM MYSTERIUM

GILES SWAYNE
(b.1946)
Op.45

83

12.xi.1986

# 21. THE CRADLE IN BETHLEHEM

Text
Rodney Bennett

ROGER QUILTER
(1877-1953)

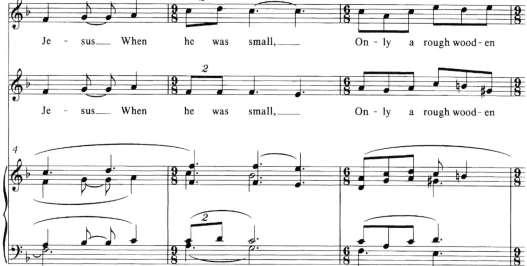

man - ger___ In a poor stall;___ Yet the

man - ger In___ a poor stall;___ Yet the

ba - by who lay there so low - ly___ Was king of us

ba - by who lay there, low - ly, so low - ly Was king of us

**poco rit.**

**a tempo** **poco rit.** **a tempo** *pp*

all.___ There was no lamp in the

all.___ There was no lamp in the

**a tempo** **poco rit.** **a tempo**

# 22. THE LAMB

from *Four Songs of Innocence*

Text
William Blake

H. WALFORD DAVIES
(Op.4 no.1)
(1869-1941)

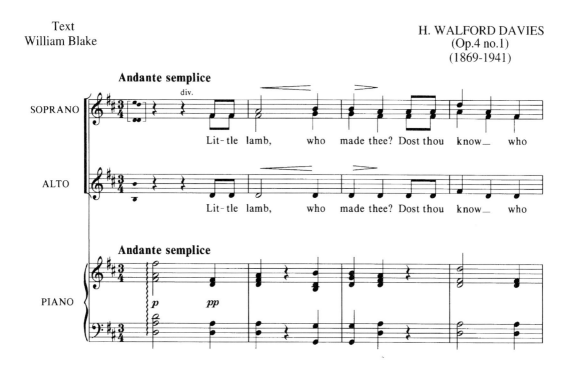

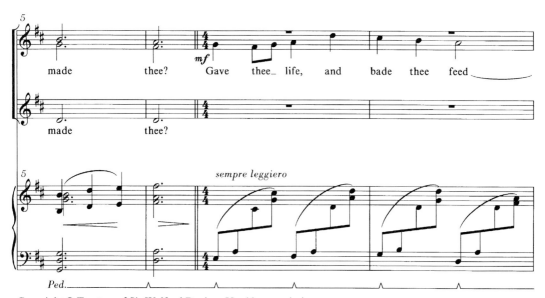

*For The Mall School, Twickenham*

# 23. PRAISE THE LORD

Text
Psalm 150**

CAROL BARRATT
(b. 1945)

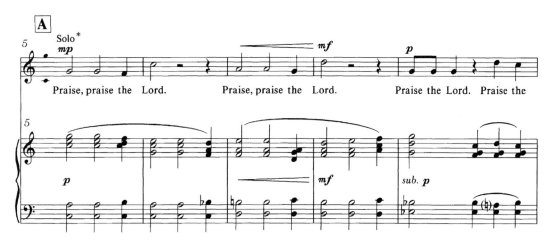

\* Solo or a few voices  † An arrangement for brass quintet is available on hire.

© Copyright 1997 Novello & Company Limited

** Words from the *Good News Bible,* Copyright American Bible Society, New York, 1976, 1992.
Used by permission of The Bible Society

† Optional 2 parts, or top part only

† Optional 2 parts, or top part only

*On the word "drums", roll "r's" if possible.

* Solo or a few voices
† Optional 2 parts, or top line only

100

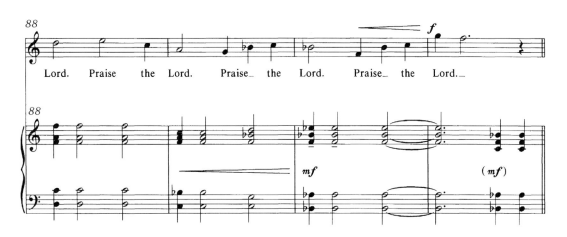

Lord. Praise the Lord. Praise the Lord. Praise the Lord.

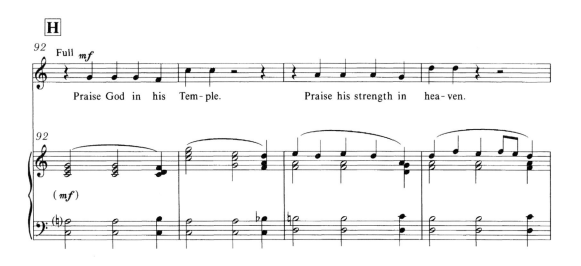

**H**

Full

Praise God in his Tem-ple. Praise his strength in hea-ven.

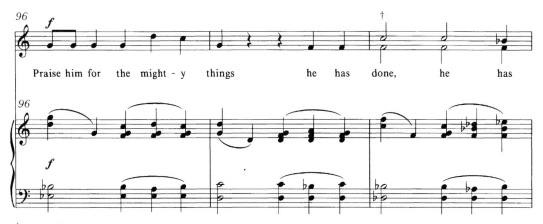

Praise him for the might-y things he has done, he has

† Optional 2 parts, or top line only.

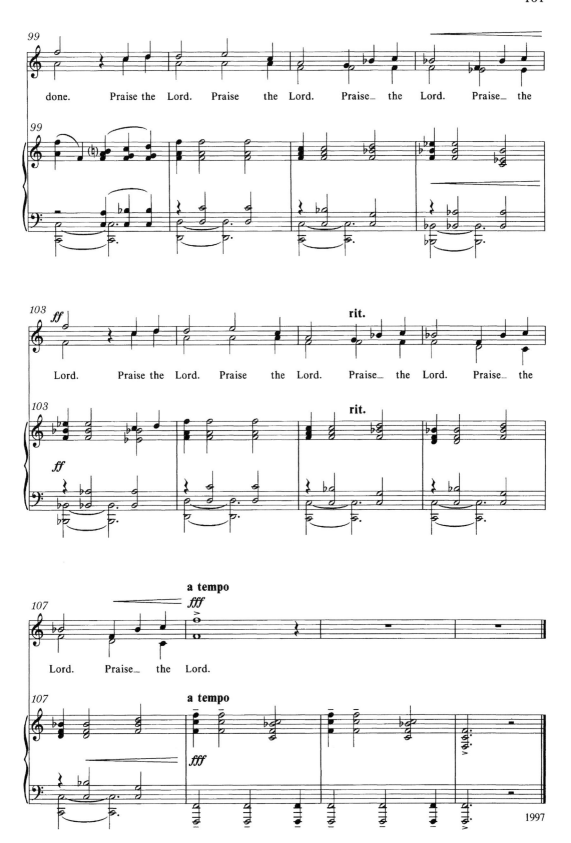

done. Praise the Lord. Praise the Lord. Praise the Lord. Praise the

Lord. Praise the Lord. Praise the Lord. Praise the Lord. Praise the

Lord. Praise the Lord.

**rit.**

**a tempo**

1997

*To the Rev. G.E. Reindorp, M.A.*
*and the choristers of St Stephen's Church, Rochester Row, S.W.1*

# 24. PREVENT US, O LORD

Text
Book of Common Prayer

DEREK HOLMAN
(b.1931)

*Written for Nick Stephenson and the choir of St Catherine's School, Richmond, Virginia*

# 25. PREVENT US, O LORD

Text
Book of Common Prayer

ALAN RIDOUT
(1934-1996)

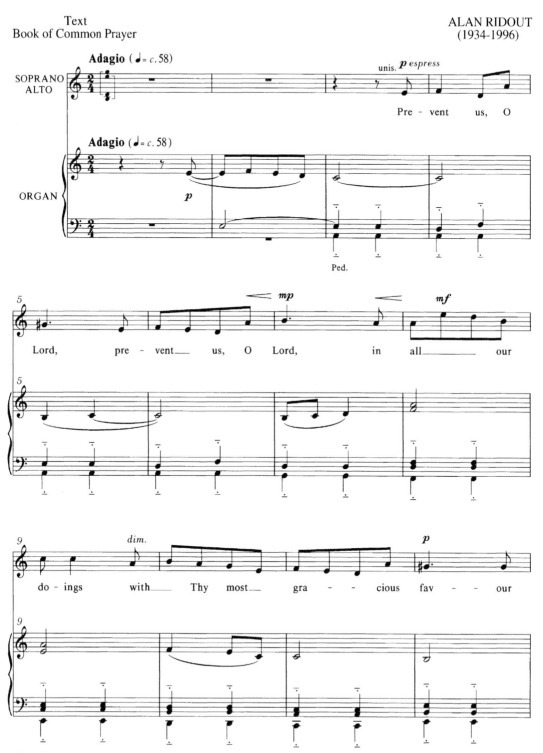

105

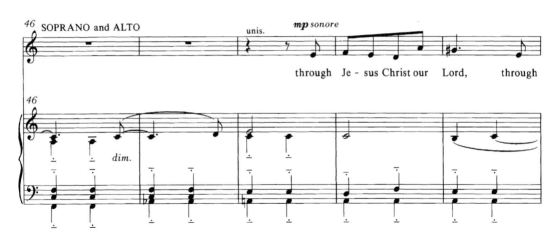

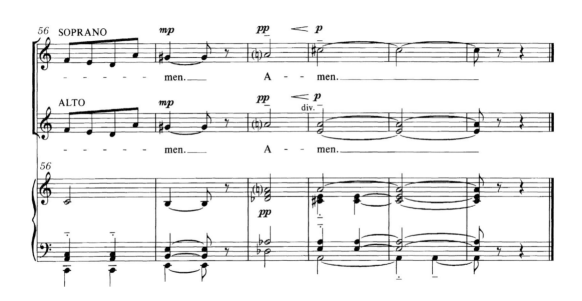

*For Edith and Colin Slee, Good Friday 1989*

# 26. RISEN LORD

Text supplied by
Rev. John Hencher

BARRY ROSE
(b.1934)

*A few voices only

# 27. THE BLESSED VIRGIN'S CRADLE SONG

### Christmas Carol

Text
Rev. Edgar Rogers

EDWARD BAIRSTOW
(1874-1946)

Born with-out a pang, While the an-gel's an – them Thro' the hea-vens

rang. Poor the wel-come bid Thee, Yet the best is nigh,

Love, the love of moth – er, Love Thy lul-la – by, Love Thy

*For the Cathedral Choristers of St. Albans*

# 28. PRECES AND RESPONSES

STEPHEN DARLINGTON
(b.1952)

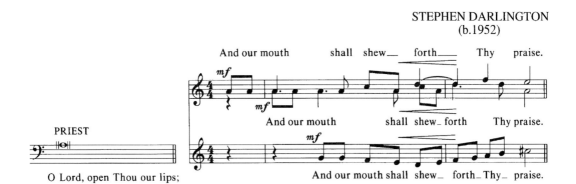

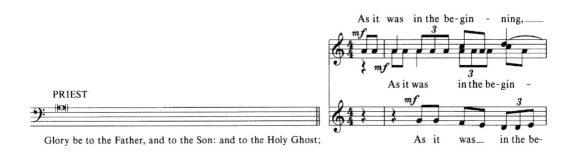

118

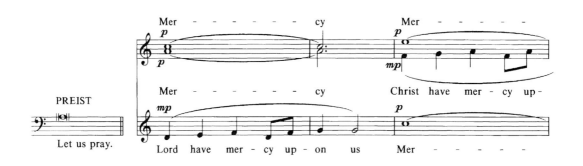

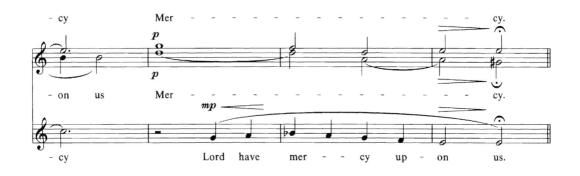

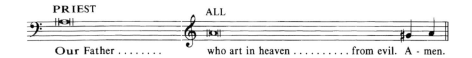

Our Father . . . . . . . . who art in heaven . . . . . . . . . from evil. A - men.

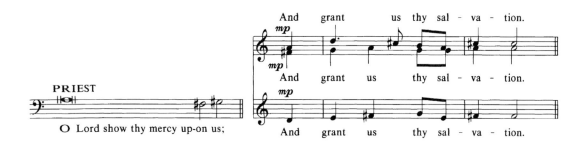

And grant us thy sal - va - tion.

And grant us thy sal - va - tion.

O Lord show thy mercy up-on us;

And grant us thy sal - va - tion.

And mer - ci - ful - ly hear us when we call up-on_ Thee.

And. mer - ci - ful - ly hear. us when we call_ up-on_ Thee.

O Lord save the Queen;

And mer-ci-ful-ly hear us when we call up - on_ Thee.

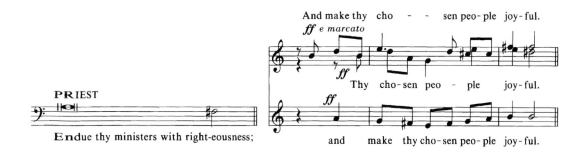

And make thy cho - - - sen peo - ple joy - ful.

Thy cho-sen peo - ple joy-ful.

Endue thy ministers with right-eousness;

and make thy cho-sen peo-ple joy-ful.

And_ bless___ thine in - he - ri - tance.___

And bless_____ thine in - he - ri - tance.___

O Lord save Thy peo-ple;

And bless_____ thine in - he - ri - tance.___

120

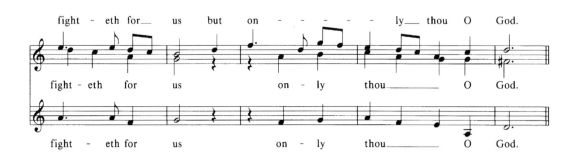

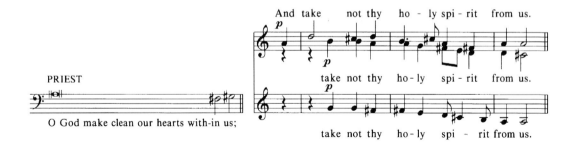

[Prayers:]
PRIEST

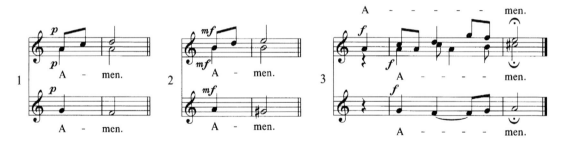

Printed and bound in Great Britain by
Caligraving Limited Thetford Norfolk